Inspirational Quotes
The Best Inspirational Quotes of Famous People and Philosophers (famous quotes, happiness quotes, motivational quotes, love quotes, funny quotes)

JOHN WALKER

CONTENTS

Chapter 1: Quotes about a Human

The measure of who we are is what we do with what we have.
Vince Lombardi

Give light, and the darkness will disappear of itself.
Desiderius Erasmus

A hero is someone who has given his or her life to something bigger than oneself.
Joseph Campbell

People seldom read a book which is given to them.
Samuel Johnson

Man never made any material as resilient as the human
spirit.
Bernard Williams

Either I will find a way, or I will make one.
Philip Sidney

It's not what a man stands for that counts, it's what he falls
for.
Tommy Dewar

Only a bad man is too courageous with women.
Michael Rusinek

Men have a touchstone whereby to try gold, but gold is the
touchstone whereby to try men.
Thomas Fuller

Mankind has perfected everything but a man.
E. McKenzie

The real man smiles in trouble, gathers strength from
distress, and grows brave by reflection.
Thomas Paine

Nothing prevents illusion as much as a thorough look in
the mirror.
Aldous Huxley

It is never too late to be what you might have been.
George Eliot

I hated every minute of training, but I said, 'Don't quit.
Suffer now and live the rest of your life as a champion.'
Muhammad Ali

The things that we love tell us what we are.
Thomas Aquinas

Out of difficulties grow miracles.
Jean de La Bruyere

Human behavior flows from three main sources: desire,
emotion, and knowledge.
Plato

Exploration is really the essence of human spirit.
Frank Borman

The human body is the best picture of the human soul.
Ludwig Wittgenstein

The two enemies of human happiness are pain and boredom.
Arthur Schopenhauer

Inside every human being there are treasures to unlock.
Mike Huckabee

Problems only exist in human mind.
Anthony de Mello

The main thing in life is not to be afraid of being human.
Aaron Carter

In order to be irreplaceable one must always be different.
Coco Chanel

The biggest changes in a women's nature are brought by love; in man, by ambition.
Rabindranath Tagore

All men are more concerned to recover what they lose than to acquire what they lack.
Aesop

Man is the only creature who refuses to be what he is.
Albert Camus

The spirit of a man is constructed out of his choices.
Irvin D. Yalom

The deepest principle in human nature is the craving to be appreciated.
William James

Chapter 2: Quotes about Life

Save your time – it's a fabric that our life is woven out of.
Samuel Richardson

My mission in life is not merely to survive, but to thrive; and to do so with some passion, some compassion, some humor, and some style.
Maya Angelou

Movies are real life with the boring parts cut out.
Alfred Hitchcock

A dream is what makes people love life even when it is painful.
Theodore Zeldin

The difference between the impossible and the possible lies in a man's determination.
Tommy Lasorda

People would rather give their life away than their money.
Emile Chartier

Don't forget until too late that the business of life is not business but living.
Bryan Forbes

The best preparation for tomorrow is doing your best today.
H. Jackson Brown, Jr.

There is nothing the busy man is less busied with than living.
Seneca.

Middle age: when you begin to exchange your emotions for symptoms.
Irvin Cobb

People say that life is the thing, but I prefer reading.
Logan Pearsall Smith

Let us sacrifice our today so that our children can have a better tomorrow.
A. P. J. Abdul Kalam

Do not take life too seriously. You will never get out of it alive.
Elbert Hubbard

The bird is powered by its own life and by its motivation.
A. P. J. Abdul Kalam

You are not here merely to make a living. You are here in order to enable the world to live more amply, with greater vision, with a finer spirit of hope and achievement. You are here to enrich the world, and you impoverish yourself if you forget the errand.
Woodrow Wilson

Smile in the mirror. Do that every morning and you'll start to see a big difference in your life.
Yoko Ono

Live life to the fullest, and focus on the positive.
Matt Cameron

The good life is one inspired by love and guided by knowledge.
Bertrand Russel

Life is really simple, but we insist on making it complicated.
Confucius

Very little is needed to make a happy life; it is all within yourself, in your way of thinking.
Marcus Aurelius

All you need in this life is ignorance and confidence, and success is sure.
Mark Twain

Love other human beings as you would love yourself.
Ho Chi Minh

Life is like riding a bicycle. To keep your balance you must move forward.
Albert Einstein

We do not remember days, we remember moments.
Cesare Pavese

Everything you can imagine is real.
Pablo Picasso

Chapter 3: Quotes about Time

The Times is speechless.
Winston Churchill

Losers are never late but they are always at the wrong time.
Don-Aminado

It is a mistake to try to look too far ahead.
Winston Churchill

Let your life lightly dance on the edges of Time like dew on the tip of a leaf. Rabindranath Tagore

One can't make his reputation on what he will do tomorrow.
E. McKenzie

There are no dark times, but there are gloomy people.
Romain Rolland

You can ask of me anything you wish except of my time.
Napoleon I

Regret for wasted time is more wasted time.
Mason Cooley

Punctuality is the politeness of kings.
Louis XVII

Today's procurement problems were yesterday's
procurement solutions.
Senator Sam Nunn

A Russian man harnesses the horse slowly but drives fast.
Otto Von Bismark

Learn from the past, set vivid, detailed goals for the future,
and live in the only moment of time over which you have
any control: now.
Denis Waitley

I am not a has-been. I am a will be.
Lauren Bacall

Don't waste your time with explanations: people only hear
what they want to hear.
Paulo Coelho

Don't spend time beating on a wall, hoping to transform it into a door.
Coco Chanel

A man must be big enough to admit his mistakes, smart enough to profit from them, and strong enough to correct them.
John C. Maxwell

Time is a created thing. To say 'I don't have time,' is like saying, 'I don't want to.
Lao Tzu

Quotes about Time and Destiny

Life is like the Olympic games; a few men strain their muscles to carry off a prize, others sell trinkets to the crowd for a profit; some just come to see how everything is done.
Pythagoras

Sometimes it takes a wrong turn to get you to the right place.
Mandy Hale

Between depriving a man of one hour from his life and depriving him of his life there exists only a difference of degree.
Frank Herbert

You could not step twice into the same river
Heraclitus of Ephesus

Each player must accept the cards life deals him or her: but once they are in hand, he or she alone must decide how to play the cards in order to win the game.
Voltaire

Be reverent before the dawning day. Do not think of what will be in a year, or in ten years. Think of today.
Roman Roland

Rought fate may be compensation for personal mediocrity.
Gary Romain

I think 'destiny' is just a fancy word for a psychological pattern.
Jodie Foster

Fate is not satisfied with inflicting one calamity.
Publilius Syrus

Two of the greatest tyrants in the world: the case and the time.
Johann Herder

There's nowhere you can be that isn't where you're meant to be...
John Lennon

The only person you are destined to become is the person you decide to be.
Ralph Waldo Emerson

Some things are destined to be - it just takes us a couple of tries to get there.
J.R. Ward, Lover Mine

Destiny is a name often given in retrospect to choices that had dramatic consequences.
Joanne Rowling

Destiny is not a matter of chance; it is a matter of choice. It is not a thing to be waited for, it is a thing to be achieved.
William Jennings Bryan

Sometimes the dreams that come true are the dreams you never even knew you had.
Alice Sebold, The Lonely Bones

If you do not change direction, you may end up where you are heading
Gautma Buddha

Realize that if a door closed, it's because what was behind it wasn't meant for you.
Mandy Hale

Character is destiny.
Heraclitus

We ought to face our destiny with courage.
Friedrich Nietzsche

What's meant to be will always find a way.
Trisha Yearwood

Time and tide wait for no man.
Stephen King

It is not in the stars to hold our destiny but in ourselves.
William Shakespeare

There are no wrong turnings. Only paths we had not
known we were meant to walk.
Guy Gavriel Kay

The foolish man seeks happiness in the distance. The wise
grows it under his feet.
James Oppenheim

Control your own destiny or someone else will.
Jack Welch

A person often meets his destiny on the road he took to
avoid it.
Jean de La Fontaine

Time you enjoy wasting is not wasted time.
Marthe Troly-Curtin

Don't spend time beating on a wall, hoping to transform it
into a door.
Coco Chanel

Quotes about Age

Youth is a disease from which we all recover.
Johann Wolfgang Goethe

No, that is the great fallacy: the wisdom of old men. They do not grow wise. They grow careful.
Ernest Hemingway

Adolescence is a period of rapid changes. Between the ages of 12 and 17, for example, a parent ages as much as 20 years.
Anonymous

A man is young when he is not afraid of doing stupid things.
Peter Kapitsa

The afternoon knows what the morning never suspected.
Robert Frost

Almost everything that is great has been done by youth.
Benjamin Disraeli

If you want to recapture your youth, just cut off his
allowance.
Al Bernstein

Count you years in money and you will see how little it is.
Magdalena Impostor Cielecka

Nothing is more responsible for the good old days than a
bad memory.
Franklin Adams

Wealth in old age is the continuation of youth.
Charles Lamb

I know not age, nor weariness nor defeat.
Rose Kennedy

Age does not protect you from love. But love, to some
extent, protects you from age.
Anais Nin

A diplomat is a man who always remembers a woman's birthday but never remembers her age.
Robert Frost

When I have the two greatest stimulants in the world to action, Youth and Debt.
Benjamin Disraeli

Anyone who stops learning is old, whether at twenty or eighty. Anyone who keeps learning stays young. The greatest thing in life is to keep your mind young.
Henry Ford

Education is the best provision for old age.
Aristotle

And the beauty of a woman, with passing years only grows!
Audrey Hepburn

At 50, everyone has the face he deserves.
George Orwell

You don't stop laughing when you grow old, you grow old when you stop laughing.
George Bernard Shaw

One's destination is never a place, but a new way of seeing things.
Henry Miller

Wrinkles should merely indicate where the smiles have been.
Mark Twain

Chapter 4: Quotes about Friendship

If you live with a cripple, you will learn to limp.
Plutarch

Friendship between women is just a non-aggression pact.
Henry de Montherlant

The rule of friendship means there should be mutual sympathy between them, each supplying what the other lacks and trying to benefit the other, always using friendly and sincere words.
Marcus Tullius Cicero

My best friend is the man who in wishing me well wishes it for my sake.
Aristotle

There are no friends at cards or world politics.
Finley Peter Dunne

The best way to keep your friends is not to give them away.
Mizner

Never judge a person by his friends. Judah had perfect friends.
Paul Valery

He who has many friends, does not have a single friend.
Aristotle

Friends stay friends longer if you test them less.
E. McKenzie

Friendship may, and often does, grow into love, but love never subsides into friendship.
Lord Byron

One of the most beautiful qualities of true friendship is to understand and to be understood.
Lucius Annaeus Seneca

A friend is someone who gives you total freedom to be yourself.

Jim Morrison

One loyal friend is worth ten thousand relatives.
Euripides

My best friend is the man who in wishing me well wishes it
for my sake.
Aristotle

True friendship is like sound health; the value of it is
seldom known until it is lost.
Charles Caleb Colton

Friendship is the hardest thing in the world to explain. It's
not something you learn in school. But if you haven't
learned the meaning of friendship, you really haven't
learned anything.
Muhammad Ali

Find a group of people who challenge and inspire you; spend a lot of time with them, and it will change your life.
Amy Poehler

A friend is one that knows you as you are, understands where you have been, accepts what you have become, and still, gently allows you to grow.
William Shakespeare

Wishing to be friends is quick work, but friendship is a slow-ripening fruit.
Aristotle

Friendship is the only cement that will ever hold the world together.
Woodrow T. Wilson

Friendship consists in forgetting what one gives and remembering what one receives.
Alexander Dumas

No person is your friend who demands your silence, or denies your right to grow.
Alice Walker

You can make more friends in two months by becoming interested in other people than you can in two years by trying to get other people interested in you.
Dale Carnegie

There is nothing on this earth to be prized than true friendship.
Thomas Aquinas

The greatest healing therapy is friendship and love.
Hubert H. Humphrey

Things are never quite as scary when you've got a best friend.
Bill Waterson

A true friend is one who overlooks your failures and tolerates your success.
Doug Larson

Friendship is essentially a partnership.
Seneca

A friend is one who knows you and loves you just the same.
Elbert Hubbard

The only way to have a friend is to be one.
Ralph Waldo Emerson

Chapter 5: Quotes about Love and Relationship

Quotes about a Woman

Women have no age. They are either young or old.
Sacha Guitry

Nothing can be so unsteady like woman's denial.
Vittorio De Sica

A woman is frank when she does not lie uselessly.
Anatole France

When a woman is talking to you, listen to what she says
with her eyes.
Victor Hugo

I see when men love women. They give them but a little of
their lives. But women when they love give everything.
Oscar Wilde

The most difficult task for a woman is to prove a man the seriousness of his intentions.
Unknown

Every woman has two opinions: her own and wrong.
Bing Crosby

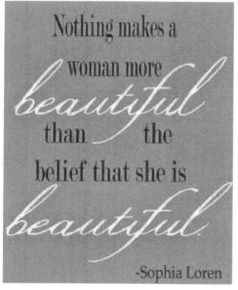

Women and cats will do as they please, and men and dogs should relax and get used to the idea.
Robert A.Heinlein

Being a woman is a terribly difficult trade since it consists principally of dealings with men.
Joseph Conrad

A witty woman is a treasure; a witty beauty is a power.
George Meredith

The true man wants two things: danger and play. For that reason he wants woman, as the most dangerous plaything.
Friedrich Nietzsche

Whatever women do they must do it twice as well as men to be thought half as good. Luckily this is not difficult.
Charlotte Whitton

You can prove a woman she is wrong but you can't persuade her in it.

John Collins

A woman forgives only when she is guilty.
Arsen Husse

If a man hasn't what's necessary to make a woman love
him, it's his fault, not hers.
W. Somerset Maugham

A woman's mind is cleaner than a man's: She changes it
more often.
Oliver Herford

There are only three things that women need in life: food,
water and compliments.
Chris Rock

Women are made to be loved, not understood.
Oscar Wilde

Women are the largest untapped reservoir of talent in the world.
Hillary Clinton

Being a woman is a terribly difficult task, since it consists principally in dealing with men.
Joseph Conrad

All the reasonings of men are not worth one sentiment of women.
Voltaire

A woman is like a tea bag – you can't tell how strong she is until you put her in hot water.
Eleanor Roosewelt

Think like a queen. A queen is not afraid to fail. Failure is another steppingstone to greatness.
Oprah Winfrey

A woman should be like a single flower, not a whole bouquet.
Anna Held

Women hold up half the sky.
Mao Zedong

The last thing left in nature is the beauty of woman.
Peter Beard

A woman's greatest asset is her beauty.
Alex Comfort

Quotes about a Man and a Woman

Women can do anything, men – the rest.
Henri de Regnier

Men mostly speak about something and women – about somebody…
Unknown

A woman's guess is much more accurate than a man's certainty.
Rudyard Kipling

Every woman's mistake has man's fault.
Johann Gottfried Herder

Every woman must remember that a man seeks a life partner but not its hostess.
Unknown

Bigamy is having one wife too many. Monogamy is the same.
Oscar Wilde

Women like children love to say "no". And men like children take it serious.
Unknown

A man does what he can; a woman does what a man cannot.
Isabel Allende, Inés of My Soul

Men and women have strengths that complement each other.
Edwin Louis Cole

Woman's wish is a law while man's wish is a woman.
Unknown

Behind every great man is a woman rolling her eyes.
Jim Carrey

A successful man is one who makes more money than his wife can spend. A successful woman is one who can find such a man.
Lana Turner

Beauty makes a slave of a man and a stinker of a woman.
Unknown

One frequently only finds out how really beautiful a women is, until after considerable acquaintance with her.
Mark Twain

Men and women are like right and left hands; it doesn't make sense not to use both.
Jeannette Rankin

Man is always looking for someone to boast to; woman is always looking for a shoulder to put her head on.
Henry Louis Mencken

As lovers, the difference between men and women is that women can love all day long, but men only at times.
W. Somerset Maugham

The difference between the love of a man and the love of a woman is that a man will always give reasons for loving, but a woman gives no reasons for loving.
Fulton J. Sheen

Women are as old as they feel and men are old when they lose their feelings.
Mae West

When men and women agree, it is only in their conclusions; their reasons are always different.
George Santayana

It's funny about men and women. Men pay in cash to get them and pay in cash to get rid of them. Women pay emotionally coming and going. Neither has it easy.
Hedy Lamarr

A woman may be able to change the world, but she will never be able to change a man.
Amy Snowden

When men and women are able to respect and accept their differences then love has a chance to blossom.
John Gray

A man is given the choice between loving women and understanding them.
Ninon de L'Enclos

Quotes about Beauty

You can never be too rich or too thin.
Wallis Simpson

The history of beautiful women is full of awful stories.
Józef Bulatović

The well-dressed man is he whose clothes you never notice.
Somerset Maugham

A beautiful woman mustn't be too smart - it distracts attention.
Marc-Gilbert Sauvajon

Fabulous women don't amaze the same for the second time.
Stendhal

Women pay their attention not to beautiful men but men with beautiful women.
Milan Kundera

Beauty…You have only a few years in which to live really, perfectly, and fully.
Oscar Wilde

Nothing makes a woman look older than obvious expensiveness, ornateness, complication.
Gabrielle Chanel

Even the most beautiful legs end somewhere.
Julian Tuwim

Kindness in women, not their beauteous looks, shall win
my love. Washington Irving

Let us leave pretty women to men with no imagination.
Marcel Proust

Everything has beauty,
but not everyone sees
it.
Confucius

Beauty is power; a
smile is its sword.
John Ray

Beauty awakens the
soul to act.
Dante Alighieri

What you do, the way
you think, makes you
beautiful.
Scott Westerfeld

Everything has beauty, but not everyone sees it.
Confucius

Crying is for plain women. Pretty women go shopping.
Oscar Wilde

The truth is not always beautiful, nor beautiful words the

truth.
Lao Tzu

There are no bad pictures; that's just how your face looks sometimes.
Abraham Lincoln

You can be gorgeous at thirty, charming at forty, and irresistible for the rest of your life.
Coco Chanel

Beauty is how you feel inside, and it reflects in your eyes. It is not something physical.
Sophia Loren

Beauty is no quality in things themselves: It exists merely in the mind which contemplates them; and each mind perceives a different beauty.
David Hume

Beauty is the illumination of your soul.
John O'Donohue

Strangeness is a necessary ingredient in beauty.
Charles Baudelaire

Quotes about Love

A happy love is full of quarrels, you know.
Jean Anouilh

Love is the best way to overcome embarrassment.
Sigmund Freud

To love a person for beauty is the same as to like chocolate
for a cover.
Unknown

Love to a neighbor is not love to a girl next door.
Thomas Hobbes

If you love somebody, let them go, for if they return, they
were always yours. And is they don't, they never were.
Khalil Gibran

Love is when the other person's happiness is more important than your own.
H. Jackson Brown, Jr.

Being deeply loved by someone gives you strength, while loving someone deeply gives you courage.
Lao Tzu

Never make a decision when you are upset, sad, jealous, or in love.
Mario Teguh

Love of beauty is taste. The creation of beauty is art.
Ralph Waldo Emerson

The best thing to hold onto in life is each other. Audrey Hepburn

Life is too long for love only.
Erich Maria Remarque

A woman knows sense of love, man – its price.
Martti Larni

A flower cannot blossom without sunshine, and man cannot live without love.
Max Mulller

Love yourself. It is important to stay positive because beauty comes from the inside out.
Jenn Proske

True love stories never have endings.
Richard Bach

Love is the flower you've got to let grow.
John Lennon

With love and patience, nothing is impossible.
Daisaku Ikeda

Quotes about Unfaithfulness and Jealousy

In everything, satiety closely follows the greatest pleasures.
Marcus Tullius Cicero

When a woman does not know what she wants that means she wants not you.
Arkady Davidovich

Jealous husband equals betrayed husband.
Marcel Proust

A man is jealous to those ones before him, a woman – who will be after her.
Marcel Achard

Jealousy is a fear of other's domination.
Alexandre Dumas, fils

Little jealousy strengthens love, big one – destroys.
Unknown

A jealous husband doesn't doubt his wife, but himself.
Honore De Balzac

The only way to get rid of a temptation is to yield to it.
Oscar Wilde

Actually, there are only two perversions: hockey on grass and ballet on ice.
Oscar Wilde

Love looks through a telescope; envy, through a microscope.
Josh Billings

Our envy always lasts longer than the happiness of those we envy.
Heraclitus

There is never jealousy where there is not strong regard.
Washington Irving

Jealousy is the fear of comparison.
Max Frisch

Quotes about Marriage

Where there is marriage without love, there will be love without marriage.
Benjamin Franklin

Marriage is a fever that starts with hot and ends with cold.
Hippocrates

Wayne: Garth, marriage is punishment for shoplifting in some countries.
Wayne's World

Unmarried man is still a boy till the end of his days.
Leo Tolstoy

Marriage was not invented by nature.
Napoleon

No man will live with a woman who respects his kindness.
Lillian Hellman

It is a bigger mercy in marriage to love than to be loved.
Plutarch

Grief at the absence of a loved one is happiness compared
to life with a person one hates.
Jean De La Bruyere

Love is the extremely difficult realization that something
other than oneself is real.
Iris Murdoch

If you are afraid of solitude then don't get married!
Anton Chekhov

Love doesn't make the world go round. Love is what
makes the ride worthwhile.
Franklin P. Jones

In dreams and in love there are no impossibilities.
Janos Arnay

To find someone who will love you for no reason, and to shower that person with reasons, that is the ultimate happiness.
Robert Brault

Success in marriage does not come merely through finding the right mate, but through being the right mate.
Barnett Brickner

A successful marriage requires falling in love many times, always with the same person.
Mignon McLaughlin

A happy marriage is a long conversation which always seems too short.
Andre Maurois

When a wife has a good husband it is easily seen in her face.
Johann Wolfgang Von Goethe

A marriage without conflicts is almost as inconceivable as a nation without crises.
Andre Maurois

Happiness in marriage is entirely a matter of chance.
Jane Austen

The value of marriage is not that adults produce children, but that children produce adults.
Peter De Vries

Quotes about Happiness

Sometimes you need to fight with yourself to get happiness.
Unknown

Happiness is not something you postpone for the future; it is something you design for the present.
Jim Rohn

True happiness is... to enjoy the present, without anxious dependence upon the future. Lucius
Annaeus Seneca

A woman must be a genius to create a good husband.
Honore de Balzac

Whoever is happy will make others happy too.
Anne Frank

The more problems a man has the less he needs for happiness.
Unknown

Happy is the man who finds a true friend, and far happier is he who finds that true friend in his wife.
Franz Schubert

Happiness is a butterfly, which when pursued, is always just beyond your grasp, but which, if you will sit down quietly, may alight upon you.
Nathaniel Hawthorne

Money give people everything what others who haven't it call happiness
Henri Joehanson

Happiness is when people understand you; misfortune is when you are rumbled…
Unknown

Each person has his or her own plan of life - what is good may vary.
John Rawls

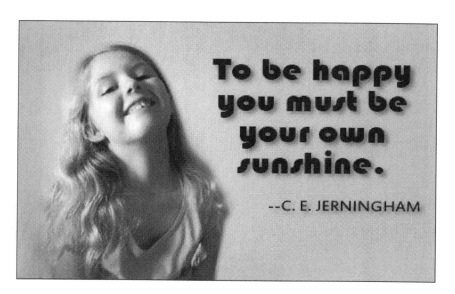

Keep your eyes wide open before marriage, and half-shut afterwards.
Benjamin Franklin

Happiness is when the desired coincides with inevitable.
Unknown

Happiness is not an ideal of reason but of imagination.
Immanuel Kant

To look forward to pleasure is also a pleasure.
Gotthold Lessing

True happiness involves the full use of one's power and talents.
John W. Gardner

For every minute you are angry you lose sixty seconds of happiness.
Ralph Waldo Emerson

Stop comparing yourself to other people, just choose to be happy and live your own life.
Roy T. Bennett

Folks are usually about as happy as they make their minds up to be.
Abraham Lincoln

Happiness is when what you think, what you say, and what you do are in harmony.
Mahatma Gandhi

Be happy for this moment. This moment is your life.
Omar Khayyam

Happiness doesn't depend on any external conditions, it is governed by our mental attitude.
Dale Carnegie

The most simple things can bring the most happiness.
Izabella Scorupco

I do believe that if you haven't learnt about sadness, you cannot appreciate happiness.
Nana Mouskouri

Happiness is not something ready made. It comes from your own actions.
Dalai Lama XIV

You will never be happy if you continue to search for what happiness consists of. You will never live if you if you are looking for a meaning of life.
Albert Camus

Happiness depends upon ourselves.
Aristotle

The measure of success is happiness and peace in mind.
Bobby Davro

Marriage is the most natural state of man, and… the state in which you will find solid happiness.
Benjamin Franklin

Learn to value yourself, which means: fight for your happiness.
Ayn Rand

The best way to cheer yourself is to try to cheer someone else up.
Mark Twain

All happiness depends on courage and work.
Honore de Balzac

One of the keys to happiness is a bad memory.
Rita Mae Brown

The happiness of your life depends upon the quality of your thoughts.
Marcus Aurelius

Happiness is not the absence of problems, it's the ability to deal with them.
Steve Maraboli

Happiness is the meaning and the purpose of life, the whole aim and end of human existence.
Aristotle

Don't waste your time in anger, regrets, worries, and grudges. Life is too short to be unhappy.
Roy T. Bennett

The secret of happiness is freedom, the secret of freedom is courage.
Carrie Jones

There are two ways to get enough. One is to continue to accumulate more and more. The other is to desire less.
G.K. Chesterton

Whoever is happy will make others happy.
Anne Frank

The problem with people is they forget that most of the time it's the small things that count.
Jennifer Niven

Very little is needed to make a happy life; it is all within yourself in your way of thinking.
Marcus Aurelius

Happiness doesn't result from what we get, but from what we give.
Ben Carson

The only way to find true happiness is to risk being completely cut open.
Chuck Palahniuk

Chapter 6: Quotes about World and House

It's a small world.
Christopher Columbus

Order is a chaos that we got used to.
Robert Lembke

The world belongs to optimists. Pessimists are only spectators.
Francois Guizot

Accessories are stark emotions of a man.
Unknown

Change your thoughts and you change the world.
Norman Vincent Peale

The best and most beautiful things in the world cannot be seen or even touched - they must be felt with the heart.
Helen Keller

The mouse that hath but one hole is quickly taken.
George Herbert

Three removes equals a fire.
Benjamin Franklin

Nothing else makes people apart like common dwelling.
Zbigniew Holodiuk

Home is where the heart is.
Pliny the Elder

The glow of one warm thought is to me worth more than money.
Thomas Jefferson

The more man meditates upon good thoughts, the better will be his world and the world at large.
Confucius

Every day is a journey, and the journey itself is home.
Matsuo Basho

A man travels the world over in search of what he needs
and returns home to find it.
George A. Moore

He is the happiest, be he king or peasant, who finds peace
in his home.
Johann Wolfgang von Goethe

Every day is a journey, and the journey itself is home.
Matsuo Basho

If you want to conquer fear, don't sit at home and think
about it. Go out and get busy.
Dale Carnegie

Chapter 7: Quotes about Art

There are no little roles, there are little actors.
Konstantin Stanislavsky

Art is the lie that enables us to realize the truth.
Pablo Picasso

Cinema films death at work.
Jean-Luc Godard

This world is a comedy for those who think and a tragedy for those who feel.
Horace Walpole

Learn art form those who earn money on that.
Samuel Butler

Every child is an artist. The problem is how to remain an artist once he grows up.
Pablo Picasso

The more the author's views are hidden the better for the work of art.
Friedrich Engels

True art advances time.
Saint-Pol-Roux

When love and skill work together, expect a masterpiece.
John Ruskin

Only that actor is great who can make public forget about their problems.
Sarah Bernhardt

When an actor is bad, applause makes him worse.
Jules Renard

The most useful of all arts is art to like.
Philip Chesterfield

All sincere feelings are bad performed.
Alexandre Dumas, fils

Art is born of the observation and investigation of nature.
Cicero

I dream my painting and I paint my dream.
Vincent van Gogh

Art enables us to find ourselves and lose ourselves at the
same time.
Thomas Merton

Life doesn't imitate art, it imitates bad television.
Woody Allen

Every portrait that is painted with feeling is a portrait of the
artist, not of the sitter.
Oscar Wilde

Art should comfort the disturbed and disturb the
comfortable.
Banksy

What I like about photographs is that they capture a
moment that's gone forever, impossible to reproduce.
Karl Lagerfeld

The painter has the Universe in his mind and hands.
Leonardo da Vinci

Art washes away from the soul the dust of everyday life.
Pablo Picasso

Creativity takes courage.
Henri Matisse

I don't paint dreams or nightmares, I paint my own reality.
Frida Kahlo

Art is what you can get away with.
Andy Warhol

Art is the only serious thing in the world. And the artist is the only person who is never serious.
Oscar Wilde

Learn the rules like a pro, so you can break them like an artist.
Pablo Picasso

One can have no smaller or greater mastery than mastery of oneself.
Leonardo da Vinci

Imagination governs the world.
Napoleon Bonaparte

The beautiful is always bizarre.
Charles Baudelaire

Music produces a kind of pleasure which human nature cannot do without.
Confucius

Life is a blank canvas, and you need to throw all the paint on it you can.
Danny Kaye

Take your broken heart, make it into art.
Carrie Fisher

Art washes away from the soul the dust of everyday life.
Pablo Picasso

Chapter 8: Quotes about Humour

Live fun while you have this chance.
Seneca the Younger

Brevity is the soul of wit.
William Shakespeare

If you can laugh together, you can work together.
Robert Orben

The chief enemy of creativity is good sense.
Pablo Picasso

A man isn't poor if he can still laugh.
Alfred Hitchcock

Jokes are necessary to make serious work.
Aristotle

Humor is one of the elements of a genius.
Johann Wolfgang von Goethe

If you want to make God laugh, tell him about your plans.
Woody Allen

It is better to joke and borrow money when nobody
expects.
Heinrich Heine

A rich man's joke is
always funny.
William Shakespeare

We participate in a
tragedy; at a comedy we
only look.
Aldous Huxley

The only way to survive
is to have a sense of
humour.
Bob Newhart

Humour is by far the
most significant activity
of the human brain.

Edward de Bono

A day without laughter is a day wasted.
Charlie Chaplin

Laughter is the closest distance between two people.
Victor Borge

Humor is just another defense against the universe.
Mel Brooks

The duty of comedy is to correct men by amusing them.
Moliere

Humor is mankind's greatest blessing.
Mark Twain

A sense of humor is a major defense against minor troubles.
Mignon McLaughlin

A good sense of humor will get you everywhere.
Josh Bowman

Life would be tragic if it weren't funny.
Stephen Hawking

I don't trust anyone who doesn't laugh.
Maya Angelou

Humor has always been a self-defence mechanism for me.
Brooke Shields

If fate doesn't make you laugh, you just don't get the joke.
Gregory David Roberts

Life is too important to take seriously.
Corky Siegel

Everything is funny, as long as it's happening to somebody else.
Will Rogers

Chapter 9: Quotes about Mistake

The last ones are always right.
Napoleon 1

He who is good at nothing
can take up anything.
Stanisław Jerzy Lec

Repeated mistake turns into
guilt.
Publilius Syrus

Avoiding faults leads to error.
Horace

He who does nothing makes no mistakes but all his life is
one big mistake.
Désiré Mercier

You may be disappointed if you fail, but you are doomed if
you don't try.
Beverly Sills

Unrealized mistakes repeat.
Boris Paramonov

To be afraid to be mistaken is already a mistake.
Unknown

No man ever steps in the same river twice, for it's not the same river and he is not the same man.
Heraclitus

You can't solve a problem unless you first admit you have one.
Harvey Mackay

Almost all misfortunes in this life happen because of talking to idiots.
Mafia manager

From the errors of others, a wise man corrects his own.
Publilius Syrus

People who spend their time looking for the faults in others usually make no time to correct their own.
Art Jonak

Anyone who has never made a mistake has never tried anything new.
Albert Einstein

A life spent making mistakes is not only more honorable, but more useful than a life spent doing nothing.
George Bernard Shaw

Life punishes a man not for his sins but for his mistakes.
Unknown

I'm willing to admit that I may not always be right, but I am never wrong.
Samuel Goldwyn

Anyone who has never made a mistake has never tried anything new.
Albert Einstein

Expect problems and eat them for breakfast.
Alfred A. Montapert

When you fail you learn from the mistakes you made and it motivates you to work even harder.
Natalie Gulbis

Healing comes from taking responsibility to realize that it is you – and no one else that creates your thoughts, your feelings, and your action.
Peter Shepherd

The human mind is the only fundamental resource.
John F. Kennedy

Have no fear of perfection - you'll never reach it.
Salvador Dali

All men make mistakes, but a good man yields when he knows his course is wrong, and repairs the evil. The only crime is pride.
Sophocles

Chapter 10: Quotes about Belief and Hope

Religion is the pious worship of God.
Cicero

Minds struck once tend to superstition.
Tacitus

Great hopes make great men.
Thomas Fuller

God loves to help him who strives to help himself.
Aeschylus

Optimism is the faith that leads to achievement. Nothing can be done without hope and confidence.
Helen Keller

The people who influence you are the people who believe in you.
Henry Drummond

Fear created the first gods in the world.
Statius

Historical development of religions is in its progressive disappearance.
Joseph Dietzgen

Believe you can and you're halfway there.
Theodore Roosevelt

Waste no time arguing about what a good man should be. Be one.
Marcus Aurelius

It is during our darkest moments that we must focus to see the light.
Aristotle Onassis

Religion dies without power, power without religion is not active.
Mohammed Azzahiri As-Samarkandi

Ignorance is the first of premise of belief so the church values it so much.
Paul Holbach

What I am looking for is a blessing not in disguise.
Jerome K. Jerome

I don't believe you have to be better than everybody else. I believe you have to be better than you ever thought you could be.
Ken Venturi

Religious views make a nice excuse to let people act bad.
Richard Aldington

Religion and virtue has nothing in common.
Claude Adrien Helvétius

Devotion is real school of insincerity.
Jean Salaville

To doubt Gods existence means to believe in him.
Honore de Balzac

Prayer is man's greatest power!
W. Clement Stone

Believe in yourself! Have faith in your abilities! Without a humble but reasonable confidence in your own powers you cannot be successful or happy.
Norman Vincent Peale

Many of life's failures are people who did not realize how close they were to success when they gave up.
Thomas Edison

Faith is taking the first step even when you don't see the whole staircase.
Martin Luther King, Jr.

The foundation stones for a balanced success are honesty, character, integrity, faith, love, and loyalty.
Zig Ziglar

Optimism is the faith that leads to achievement. Nothing can be done without hope and confidence.
Hellen Keller

Be faithful in small things because it is in them that your strength lies.
Mother Teresa

We are twice armed if we fight with faith.
Plato

Yesterday is history, tomorrow is a mystery, today is a gift of God, which is why we call it the present.
Bil Keane

Blessed is he who expects nothing, for he shall never be disappointed.
Alexander Pope

In a time of destruction, create something.
Maxine Hong Kingston

When you have lost hope, you have lost everything. And when you think all is lost, when all is dire and bleak, there is always hope.
Pittacus Lore

Hope is a waking dream.
Aristotle

Do not spoil what you have by desiring what you have not; remember that what you now have was once among the things you only hoped for.
Epicurus

Hope is a good breakfast, but it is a bad supper.
Francis Bacon

Never lose hope. Storms make people stronger and never last forever.
Roy T. Bennett

We must accept finite disappointment, but never lose infinite hope.
Martin Luther King, Jr.

The first duty of a man is to think for himself.
Jose Marti

Keep your best wishes, close to your heart and watch what happens.
Tony DeLiso

When you're at the end of your rope, tie a knot and hold on.
Theodore Roosevelt

There is nothing like a dream to create the future.
Victor Hugo

If at first the idea is not absurd, then there is no hope for it.
Albert Einstein

Anything under God's control is never out of control.
Charles R. Swindoll

We promise according to our hopes and perform according to our fears.
Francois de La Rochefoucauld

Everything that is done in this world is done by hope.
Martin Luther

May your choices reflect your hopes, not your fears.
Nelson Mandela

Chapter 11: Quotes about Tactics

He conquers who endures.
Persius

It's better to play against sly than a lucky one.
French expression

Just don't give up trying to do what you really want to do.
Where there is love and inspiration, I don't think you can
go wrong.
Ella Fitzgerald

Great results, can be achieved with small forces.
Sun Tzu

If you accept the expectations of others, especially negative
ones, then you never will change the outcome.
Michael Jordan

A sly man fights while a wise one yields.
Karel Čapek

Simplicity is the first condition of a good manoeuvre.
Napoleon I

Always take out a snake from its hole with some others'
hands.
Unknown

I've found that luck is quite predictable. If you want more
luck, take more chances. Be more active. Show up more
often.
Brian Tracy

Small deeds done are better than great deeds planned.
Peter Marshall

If you don't ask, you don't get.
Stevie Wonder

Don't think, just do.
Horace

It is enough to ask somebody for his weapons without saying 'I want to kill you with them'.
Niccolò Machiavelli

Compromising, you lose. Expressing compromise, you take a step to the victory.
Mafia manager

All you need is the plan, the road map, and the courage to press on to your destination.
Earl Nightingale

The undertaking of a new action brings new strength.
Richard L. Evans

Don't teach your soldiers all your tricks or you will be your own victim.
Mafia manager

Defense is inherently the stronger form of war.
Carl Clausewitz

Diplomacy: the art of restraining power.
Henry A. Kissinger

It always seems impossible until its done.
Nelson Mandela

People capitulate more often than lose.
Henry Ford

Always forgive your enemies; nothing annoys them so much.
Oscar Wilde

The supreme art of war is to subdue the enemy without fighting.
Sun Tzu

Study the past if you would define the future.
Confusius

Always focus on the front windshield and not the review mirror.
Collin Powell

The essence of strategy is choosing what not to do.
Michael E. Porter

Perception is strong and sight weak. In strategy it is important to see distant things as if they were close and to take a distanced view of close things.
Miyamoto Musashi

If you can not do great things, Do small things in a great way.
Napoleon Hill

Strategy requires thought, tactics require observation.
Max Euwe

Tactics means doing what you can with what you have.
Saul Alinsky

One of the primary tactics for enduring winning is daily learning.
Robin Sharma

Chapter 12: Quotes about Education

Those who know, do. Those that understand, teach.
Aristotle

Science is a cemetery of dead ideas.
Henri Poincaré

Write right even if they dictate wrong.
Józef Bulatović

If a man neglects education, he walks lame to the end of his life.
Plato

Road without barriers usually leads nowhere.
DeFalco

With self-discipline most anything is possible.
Theodore Roosevelt

The education of a man is never completed until he dies.
Robert E. Lee

School prepares us for living in a world that doesn't exist.
Albert Camus

Perhaps the most valuable result of all education is the
ability to make yourself do the thing you have to do, when
it ought to be done, whether you like it or not.
Aldous Huxley

A poor student is a student who doesn't exceed his teacher.
Leonardo da Vinci

Knowledge gained for payment stay longer.
Rabbi Nachman

Study is learning rules, experience is learning exceptions.
Leonard Louis Levinson

The great aim of education is not knowledge but action.
Herbert Spencer

He who opens a school door, closes a prison.
Victor Hugo

Only the educated are free.
Epictetus

Education is not preparation for life; education is life itself.
John Dewey

Always desire to learn something useful.
Sophocles

Education's purpose is to replace an empty mind with an open one.
Malcolm Forbes

Education is the passport to the future, for tomorrow belong to those who prepare for it today.
Malcolm X

An investment in knowledge pays the best interest.
Benjamin Franklin

Education is the most powerful weapon which you can use to change the world.
Nelson Mandela

The aim of education is the knowledge, not of facts, but of values.
William S. Burroughs

You are educated when you have the ability to listen to almost anything without losing your temper or self-confidence.
Robert Frost

Education is what remains after one has forgotten what one has learned in school.
Albert Einstein

Change is the end result of all true learning.
Leo Buscaglia

The roots of education are bitter, but the fruit is sweet.
Aristotle

Education comes from within; you get it by struggle and effort and thought.
Napoleon Hill

Don't limit a child to your own learning, for he was born in another time.
Rabindranath Tagore

Don't let schooling interfere with your education.
Mark Twain

Nature has always had more force than education.
Voltaire

Education is an ornament in prosperity and a refuge in adversity.
Aristotle

Good manners will open doors that the best education cannot.
Clarence Thomas

All real education is the architecture of the soul.
William Bennett

The only person who is educated is the one who has learned how to learn and change.
Carl Rogers

You are always a student, never a master. You have to keep moving forward.
Conrad Hall

The highest result of education is tolerance.
Helen Keller

There is no greater education than one that is self-driven.
Neil deGrasse Tyson

The direction in which education starts a man will determine his future in life.
Plato

The whole purpose of education is to turn mirrors into windows.
Sydney J. Harris

Chapter 13: Quotes about a Word

Everyone hears only what he understands.
Johann Wolfgang von Goethe

Oratory is art of expression others' thoughts.
Edouard Herriot

To speak without thinking is like shooting without aim.
Miguel de Cervantes

If you want your report to be read write it on one page.
Woodrow Wilson

He who has what to say is always silent.
Pablo Escobar

The limits of my language means the limits of my world.
Ludwig Wittgenstein

When in doubt tell the truth.
Mark Twain

Nothing is impossible, the word itself says 'I'm possible'!
Audrey Hepburn

No matter what people tell you, words and ideas can
change the world.
Robin Williams

Those who cannot attack the thought, instead attack the
thinker.
Paul Valéry

Sincere words do not sound nice,
Nice-sounding words are not sincere.
Lao Tzu

Only truth is rude.
Napoleon

You aren't learning anything when you're talking.
Lyndon Johnson

Quotes about Explanations

If you can't convince them, confuse them.
Harry S. Truman

In fact, explanations are excuses.
Bertolt Brecht

Don't explain much if you want to be understandable.
Denis Diderot

Several excuses are always less convincing than one.
Aldous Huxley

To apologize in advance is to blame yourself.
Balthasar Gracian

Not every question deserves an answer.
Cyrus

Obviousness diminishes proofs.
Marcus Tullius Cicero

It's not information it's intonation that convinces.
Sylvia Chiz

Rational arguments have never convinced anybody.
Anatole France

Don't waste your time with explanations: people only hear
what they want to hear.
Paulo Coelho

Love is an endless mystery, because there is no reasonable
cause that could explain it.
Rabindranath Tagore

Never explain — your friends do not need it and your
enemies will not believe you anyway.
Elbert Hubbard

The only correct actions are those that demand no
explanation and no apology.
Red Auerbach

Always keep your smile. That's how I explain my long life.
Jeanne Calment

To rush into explanations is always a sign of weakness.
Agatha Christie

An explanation of cause is not a justification by reason.
C.S. Lewis

Good luck needs no explanation.
Shirley Temple

Never complain and never explain.
Benjamin Disraeli

If you can't explain it simply, you don't understand it well
enough.
Albert Einstein

Always keep your smile. That's how I explain my long life.
Jeanne Calment

Character is that sum total of moments we can't explain.
George Saunders

Two things define you: Your patience when you have
nothing and your attitude when you have everything.
Imam Ali

I think you can have 10,000 explanations for failure, but
not good explanation for success.
Paolo Coelho

Do not seek the because – in love there is no because, no
reason, no explanation, no solutions.
Anais Nin

Never waste your time trying to explain who you are to
people who are committed to misunderstanding you.
Dream Hampton

The only correct actions are those that demand no
explanation and no apology.
Red Auerbach

Chapter 14: Quotes about Talent and Genius

In order to be irreplaceable one must always be different.
Coco Chanel

Genius, in truth, means little more than the faculty of
perceiving in an unhabitual way.
William James

Talent is like a lust. It is hard to conceal it and it's even
harder to simulate.
Sergey Dovlatov

Concealed talent brings no reputation.
Erasmus Roterodamus

Your talent is God's gift to you. What you do with it is your gift back to God.
Leo Buscaglia

It's impossible to falsify three things: erection, competence and creative thinking.
Unknown

All great discoveries are made by men whose feelings run ahead of their thinking.
Charles Henry Parkhurst

It's nice to talk with a talented person but not to work.
Unknown

Contest is food for genius.
Voltaire

Genius is a man who can differ difficult from impossible.
Napoleon I

Talent without working hard is nothing.
Christiano Ronaldo

Any man can make mistakes, but only an idiot persists in his error.
Marcus Tullius Cicero

Everyone has talent. What's rare is the courage to follow it to the dark places where it leads.
Erica Jong

Talent hits a target no one else can hit. Genius hits a target no one else can see.
Arthur Schopenhauer

Talent is cheaper than table salt. What separates the talented individual from the successful one is a lot of hard work.
Stephen King

Hard work beats talent when talent fails to work hard.
Kevin Durant

Talent is a long patience, and originality an effort of will and intense observation.
Gustave Flaubert

Every talent must unfold itself in fighting.
Friedrich Nietzsche

Talent wins game, but teamwork and intelligence wins championships.
Michael Jordan

Self-doubt kills talent.
Eddie McClurg

Let the path be open to talent.
Napoleon Bonaparte

Your talent is God's gift to you. What you do with it is your gift back to God.
Leo Buscaglia

Chapter 15: Quotes about Food and Wine

There must be temperance in everything: drink, food, love.
Hippocrates

Thou shouldst eat to live; not live to eat.
Socrates.

The appetite grows by eating.
François Rabelais

Nobody is lonely when he eats spaghetti.
Unknown

At times, medicine is more dangerous than illness.
Seneca

He who loves not wine, women and song remains a fool
his whole life long.
Martin Luther

It's late to look for salt when food is eaten.
Unknown

To a man with an empty stomach food is God.
Mahatma Gandhi

He that drinks fast pays slow.
Benjamin Franklin

If more of us valued food and cheer and song above
hoarded gold, it would be a merrier world.
J.R.R. Tolkien

Let food be thy medicine and medicine be thy food.
Hippocrates

A fit, healthy body — that is the best fashion statement.
Jess C. Scott

You are what what you eat eats.
Michael Pollan

All sorrows are less with bread.
Miguel de Cervantes Saavedra

Knowledge is the food of the soul.
Plato

Quotes about Alcohol and Smoking

Intoxication is a free-will madness.
Aristotle

A clever man drinks until he feels good; a fool drinks until
he feels bad.
Unknown

A man's true character comes out when he's drunk.
Charlie Chaplin

Alcohol is a supplier of people to the prisons.
Henri Baudrillart

Smoking is a useful habit… for death.
Alexander Borovik

Alcohol takes more lives than any severe epidemic.
Karl Ernst von Baer

A beautiful woman with a cigarette looks like a rose
hammered with a nail.
Unknown

There is no other method for making idiots than alcohol.
Emil Kraepelin

Alcoholism is when you drink more than your doctor.
Unknown

Wine is constant proof that God loves us and loves to see us happy.
Benjamin Franklin

Accept what life offers you and try to drink from every cup. All wines should be tasted; some should only be sipped, but with others, drink the whole bottle.
Paulo Coelho, Brida

If more of us valued food and cheer and song above hoarded gold, it would be a merrier world.
J.R.R. Tolkien

Wine makes a man more pleased with himself; I do not say it makes him more pleasing to others.
Samuel Johnson

Always do sober what you said you'd do drunk. That will teach you to keep your mouth shut.
Ernest Hemingway

Chapter 16: Quotes about Foolishness

Impossible is a word to be found only in the dictionary of fools.
Napoleon

The trouble with the world is that the stupid are cocksure and the intelligent are full of doubt.
Bertrand Russell

Every extremity is sibling of limited nature.
Vissarion Belinsky

Lack of talent is most versatile.
Grigory Landau

A prosperous fool is a grievous burden.
Aeschylus

Silence is the virtue of fools.
Francis Bacon

A scornful look turns into a complete fool a man of
average intelligence.
Andre Maurois

I could be living the best and happiest of lives if only I
were not a fool.
Johann Wolfgang von Goethe

As one grows older, one becomes wiser and more foolish.
François de La Rochefoucauld

You will do foolish things, but do them with enthusiasm.
Colette

Talk sense to a fool and he calls you foolish.
Euripides

Compromise is a stalling between two fools.
Stephen Fry

First love is only a little foolishness and a lot of curiosity.
George Bernard Shaw

A wise man gets more use from his enemies than a fool
from his friends.

Baltasar Gracian

A learned fool is more a fool than an ignorant fool.
Molière

Our wisdom comes from our experience, and our
experience comes from our foolishness.
Sacha Guitry

Foolishness is indeed the sister of wickedness.
Sophocles

Almost all new ideas have a certain aspect of foolishness
when they are first produced.
Alfred North Whitehead

Passion often makes fools of the wisest men and gives the
silliest wisdom.
François de La Rochefoucauld

First love is only a little foolishness and a lot of curiosity.
George Bernard Shaw

Better a witty fool than a foolish wit.
William Shakespeare

A wise man can learn more from a foolish question than a
fool can learn from a wise answer.
Bruce Lee

It is a profitable thing, if one is wise, to seem foolish.
Aeschylus

Chapter 17: Quotes about Information

Urgent is often mixed up with important.
André Siegfried

Never inform about your decision beforehand.
John Selden

Information is the currency of democracy.
Ralph Nader

Never believe in mirrors or newspapers.
John James Osborne

Headlines twice the size of the events.
John Galsworthy

The merely well-informed man is the most useless bore on God's earth.
Alfred North Whitehead

He that keeps an eye on everything really notices nothing.
Mark Clayman

An editor has no right to be a beginner.
Samuil Marshak

The real news is bad news.
Marshall McLuhan

Human behavior flows from three main sources: desire, emotion, and knowledge.
Plato

To know what you know and what you do not know, that is true knowledge.
Confucius

If money is your hope for independence you will never have it. The only real security that a man will have in this world is a reserve of knowledge, experience, and ability.
Henry Ford

A man of knowledge lives by acting, not by thinking about acting.
Carlos Castaneda

Accurate information is a key part of motivation.
Mary Ann Alison

Information is the currency of democracy.
Thomas Jefferson

As a general rule, the most successful man in life is the man who has the best information.
Benjamin Disraeli

Do not seek for information of which you cannot make use.
Anna Brackett

Information is not knowledge.
Albert Einstein

Information is only useful when it can be understood.
Muriel Cooper

The mind can be convinced, but the heart must be won.
Simon Sinek

Knowledge is power. Information is liberating. Education is the premise of progress, in every society, in every family.
Kofi Annan

Information rules the world.
Winston Churchill

Learning is experience. Everything else is just information.
Albert Einstein

Intelligence plus character - that is the true goal of
education.
Martin Luther King, Jr.

Information is a negotiator's greatest weapon.
Victor Kiam

Children must be taught how to think, not what to think.
Margaret Mead

The goal is to turn data into information, and information
into insight.
Carly Fiorina

In the new economy, information, education, and
motivation are everything.
William J. Clinton

The most valuable commodity I know of is information.
Gordon Gekko

We think too much and feel too little.
Charlie Chaplin

Information in itself is not powerful; power lies at the very
core of being informed and making good use of it.
Nudi Levit

Data is what you need to do analytics. Information is what
you need to do business.
John Owen

Quotes about Intelligence and Wisdom

Intelligence seldom makes people rich but wealth makes clever of anybody.
Ben Jonson

Wisdom is ability to refuse from perfection at the right time.
Vladimir Gorovits

What we think, we become.
Buddha

Change your thoughts and you change your world.
Norman Vincent Peale

As knowledge increases, wonder deepens.
Charles Morgan

A fool thinks himself to be wise, but a wise man knows himself to be a fool.
William Shakespeare

He who knows most has more doubts.
Enea Silvio Piccolomini

It is a man's own mind, not his enemy or foe that lures him to evil ways.
Buddha

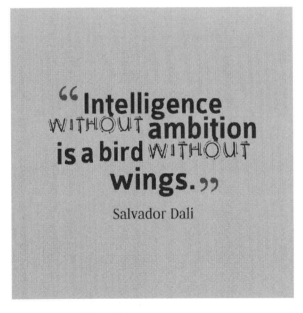

"Intelligence without ambition is a bird without wings."

Salvador Dali

All that is well planned doesn't always succeed.
Publius Syrus

The surest sign that intelligent life exists elsewhere in the universe is that it has never tried to contact us.
Bill Watterson

A wise man does not trust all his eggs to one basket.
Miguel De Cervantes

My mind's my kingdom.
Francis Quarles

A wise man will make more opportunities than he finds.
Francis Bacon

Mind is almost useless for a man who has no other
qualities.
Alexis Carrel

A clever man differs that he has ability of misunderstanding
Edouard Herriot

A clever man likes learning, a fool likes teaching.
Anton Chekhov

It is better to remain silent at the risk of being thought a
fool, than to talk and remove all doubt of it.
Maurice Switzer

Knowing yourself is the beginning of all wisdom.
Aristotle

The secret of life, though, is to fall seven times and to get
up eight times.
Paulo Coelho, The Alchemist

Where wisdom reigns, there is no conflict between thinking
and feeling.
C.G. Jung

I've come to believe that all my past failure and frustration
were actually laying the foundation for the understandings
that have created the new level of living I now enjoy.
Anthony Robbins

Look for the good in every person and every situation.
You'll almost always find it.
Brian Tracy

A home without books is a body without soul.
Marcus Tullius Cicero

The deepest principle in human nature is the craving to be
appreciated.
William James

The man is success who has lived well, laughed often and
loved much.
Robert Louis Stevenson

Thanks for reading. I hope you enjoy it. I ask you to leave your honest feedback.

I think next book will also be interesting for you:

Inspirational Quotes for Business

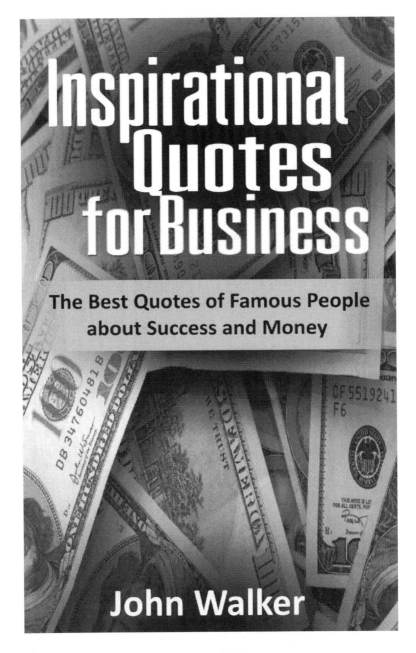